First Kiss

From The Initial Kiss To A Long-Lasting And Enduring Love A Change Of Heart: Love Transformation Through A First Kiss

(First Kiss Etiquette: Fundamental Tips And Guidance On The Art Of Kissing)

Lesley van Egmond

Emily hailed the first cab she spotted after leaving the lounge. The strong scent of air freshener made her cringe as she sank onto the cracked leather seat. She took a deep breath of fresh air and lowered her window down a bit in relief. She reclined and closed her eyes, sensing a faint headache coming on.

The driver said, glancing at her through his rearview mirror, "Where to Miss?"

Please just drive. In a moment, I'll inform you.

"All right."

The motorist started to drive at a moderate speed through the traffic. Emily leaned back, trying to regain control of her emotions as the cool breeze from the rain touched her face. She experienced disorientation, agitation, and emotional exhaustion. She felt a tear suddenly fall down her face and reached up to wipe it off.

She asked quietly in the back seat, "What's happening to me?" not caring if the driver heard her.

She clenched her hands in her lap as her thoughts focused on the cause of her uneasy nerves. She envisioned Daniel's lips pressing against hers, and the image toyed with her head. She closed her eyes, picturing the kiss growing more intense as his arms encircled her waist, narrowing the distance between them.

The driver saw a faint groan that emerged from between her parted lips.

"Miss, are you alright back there?"

Emily was startled when she heard the driver's voice, and her eyes opened wide. She was so ashamed that she momentarily lost track of her whereabouts.

"Yes, I'm alright." She decided what to do after realizing she couldn't spend the entire evening riding around in the back of the cab. Before she went completely insane, she really needed to talk to someone.

She took out her cell phone and called Stacey after seeing what time it was. Over the years, she and Stacey had grown rather close, and she needed someone to confide in. After four rings, she was about to give up until she heard her response.

"Hey?"

Emily felt calmed. "Hi, Stacey."

"Emily! How are you doing? Stacey laughed and asked. She raised her wine glass and took a small drink.

Emily truly needed someone to talk to, but she didn't want to ruin her evening. "Are you preoccupied?"

Stacey saw something in Emily's words, so she got up and walked out of the room, bringing her glass with her. She was with Tara, and they had paid Rainys' residence an unexpected visit. After dropping Jordan off earlier, Sabrina came back for his favorite toy. They were now all unwinding in the living room while sipping wine from a bottle.

"Pardon me, gentlemen. Stacey headed to the den and said, "I'm going to take this in the other room." She closed the door and then raised the phone to her ear again. "Emma, what's wrong?"

Emily began to cry once more, and she didn't give a damn whether the cabbie saw her. "I'm not sure. She sniffed, "I think I did something stupid."

As Stacey became concerned that Emily might be in danger, she began to pace back and forth. She wanted to say it aloud, but she forced herself to ask in a calm voice, "What have you done that you think is stupid?" She didn't think she would respond for a moment, but then she heard a tiny voice respond.

"I experienced love."

Stacey released the breath from her lungs, unsure of when she had begun to hold it in. Taking a big swallow of wine from her glass, she remarked, "Isn't falling in love a good thing?"

Emily forgot that Stacey couldn't see her as she nodded her head. "Yeah, but I have a man in my life."

Emily said this right as Stacey was attempting to down the wine. She spit the wine from her lips in horror at what she'd spoken. "However?" My gosh, what a mess. She patted the moisture from her shirt and thought, "I'm so glad this is white wine and not red."

Stacey collected herself and settled into a leather chair, setting the glass on a side table. Did Emily mention that she was in love with a man?

"Hmm, mm."

But, Stacey muttered, "I thought you were... gay." She did not want passersby to overhear her.

"Me too, but I haven't been interested in any ladies for the past few years. I give them no recognition at all. Rather, I've been focusing on...him.

Stacey realized Emily hadn't yet mentioned the man's name as she tried to process everything and make sense of it all. Most likely, she had met him at work. "And who is this guy you've developed feelings for?"

Emily hesitated for a while before deciding to just say it. "It's Daniel," she said with a smile, feeling relieved to have at last revealed her deepest secret to someone.

"Daniel!" Straightening her back in her chair, Stacey grinned. "Oh my god!"

Yes, you're absolutely right. How will I proceed, Stacey? He's not even aware of my feelings for him.

The news still left Stacey speechless. "Well, you should first confirm that this is truly what you want and that you're not merely experimenting."

Emily raised her hand and placed it on her chest. She felt the quick flutter of her heart against her hand. Every time her mind wandered to Daniel, she experienced the same sensation. Indeed. Without a doubt.

Excited, Stacey got to her feet. "All right, so creating a plan is the next step."

Emily smiled, a glimmer of relief from Stacey's assistance. "May I come over and have a longer chat?"

"Oh no. I'm not at my house. I'm with Tara at Rainys' place.

"Oh."

Emily's voice sounded deflated, and Stacey thought of a better strategy. With excitement, she blurted out, "You should come here." "You could use the ideas and counsel from everyone here; we're all here."

After giving it some thought, Emily hunched her shoulders. What stands to lose for me? Besides, I have no notion what to do. Alright. I'm heading there.

Grabbing her drink, Stacey made her way towards the door. Alright. I'll announce your arrival to everyone, but I won't discuss Daniel until you arrive.

The knowledge that she wouldn't be suffering in silence eased Emily's suffering. "All right, thanks, Stacey."

Emily, you're not required to thank me. I want to be there for you, just like you were there for me when I was all screwed up about Chase. Isn't that the purpose of friends, right?

Emily nodded, grinning. Indeed, it is accurate. Then, I'll see you shortly. Goodbye.

"Goodbye."

Emily was sitting smiling out the window when the call ended. I apologize, sir. Right now, I know where I want to go.

Alright. "Where to?" the man inquired, appreciating that she had at last made up her mind.

After Emily gave him Rainy's Pennsylvania address, he looked back at her in the mirror.

"Miss, that is a long drive. Do you really want to take it that far? It will cost a lot.

"Stop worrying about the price. She grinned widely and continued, "Just get me there as fast as you can without killing me."

After chuckling, the motorist switched off his on-duty light. Miss, don't worry. I recently gave birth to a baby with my wife, and I want to spend every day seeing him develop into a man.

Emily grinned and added, "I'm glad to hear that." "And congrats!"

"I'm grateful, Miss. With a broad smile, the driver said, "Thank you.

When Emily's thoughts returned to Daniel, she felt a warm glow around her, knowing that he must be thinking of his family. What does a kiss on his lips feel like?

Chapter 5: Take It All On!

You have completed the first stage of your education! It's time for you to go have that unforgettable first kiss! You are ready to take the risk because you have already assessed your partner's comfort level to make sure you both feel comfortable. Take a deep breath; this is going to be your first kiss. What scheme have you thought of for that unique occasion?

When it's time, incline closer to your companion. When you get as close as you can without risking a cross-eyed look, slowly move your face closer, turning your head slightly to avoid bumping noses, and make sure you continue to focus on their lips or eyes after giving your spouse a final look at their lips to ensure you know where you're going, carefully close your eyes and plant a kiss. Check to see if they seem interested. When you begin using your tongue, as previously mentioned, if you are both, you can proceed to the following stage. You're making out now! To help your spouse feel more at ease, back off for the time being if they are hesitant, and try again later. It is important to understand that your partner's discomfort does not equate to rejection. These two are not interchangeable. One says, "I'm not really into you," while the other says, "I'm not ready." If your partner isn't ready, you shouldn't take it personally. On the other hand, you are showcasing your maturity and self-assurance, which is a really appealing trait, by being understanding and patient. Your lover will only want to kiss you more as a result of this.

Make sure to start out with light and gentle kisses. On your first kiss, try not to be overly forceful. Gently press your lips against theirs while keeping the pressure as gentle as possible. Additionally, keep in mind that smacking too loudly can be distracting.

Additionally, you must understand where to put your hands. They have no right to be by your side. Somehow, they ought to be used throughout the kiss. Try just placing your hands on the side of your partner's face or the back of their head if you aren't already holding their hands or giving them a strong embrace. When you're kissing, go towards each other with your hands to make eye contact. You can start French kissing if you're sure your spouse is welcoming your kisses.

Part 6: How to Break Up with Someone

When you're through, you need to close your time together with them on a high note that makes them eager for your next get-together. You have to bid them farewell in a way that makes them want to kiss you again. There'll be a rush of conflicting feelings after your first kiss. Before you say goodbye, just think back to what felt really amazing and think of some positive things to say. When in doubt, say something straightforward like "I'm excited to see you again."

Ensure that your significant other is aware of how much fun you had. Try not to stress too much about your voice. Simply express your gratitude for the wonderful experience you both had. It would also be really lovely if you could give each other a tender kiss to end it. Final thoughts before you head off and after bidding me farewell.

There is no right or wrong length when it comes to kissing. The duration differs depending on the individual and the circumstances. How long you both stay in the kiss and how enthusiastic you are about it should serve as a guide for how long is right. Remain apart until your spouse is prepared to reengage if you feel like they need to get some fresh air.

It's possible that you didn't do anything improper during your first kiss. Right now, the only thing you can do is make sure it is as close to flawless as possible. You could lose your chance of receiving that first, flawless, and unforgettable kiss if you reveal to the person you want to kiss that you have been reading books about French kissing or that you have been doing the required preparations for your first time.

It's important to keep in mind that nobody is an expert when it comes to their first kiss. You should anticipate your partner to be scared as well, even if it's not their first kiss. After all, this will be their first time kissing you. You will undoubtedly kiss each other more in the future if you genuinely appreciate one another and your kiss turns out to be as passionate and ideal as you have been dreaming.

With any luck, this book will boost your self-assurance before your impending first kiss. It's definitely cause for genuine excitement! Please let me know by leaving an Amazon review if you liked the book. Regards and best of luck!

Kind of Love: What Is It?

Since this is the first time you've felt this way, you're not quite sure what to believe when you say you're in love. It's normal to compare how you're feeling to what your buddy or older sibling stated they went through. You may be confused and want to confide in someone, but you're hesitant to tell friends or family for fear of their reaction or opinion of you.

Additionally, you are aware that even if you confide in someone, their comparisons could not be the same as yours. Some youngsters detest and harass their first loves because they question whether they are sick or whether they are just going insane.

Love is a humorous thing. There are numerous forms of it. Until you really experience it, it is hard to foresee the way it will come to you. You will encounter the following types of love in a lot of romantic situations. What are you going through?

Platonic Love

The most basic kind of love is this one. Platonic love has no sexual overtones and is characterized by its extreme purity and friendliness. When you are in platonic love, you won't get butterflies in your stomach or goosebumps when you see that individual. Since platonic love is frequently reciprocal, you won't focus on why that person did not answer your phone or why they do not like you back.

The kind of affection you have with childhood friends—even those of the opposite sex—is known as platonic love. Have you ever found yourself holding something your friend gave you or hugging your teddy bear because you truly missed them? You had your first experience of platonic love at that time.

Crushes

This is a very typical teenage experience. Let's call it the first crush. Crushes are actually the universal sensation of falling in love. Nobody ever forgets the unforgettable experience of having their first crush. You instantly get perplexing jolts in your stomach and some fluttering (it feels like there are butterflies in there) when you see this certain girl or male.

You have the need to throw up. As you pass your crush, you feel like your skin has become even thinner, and you are on the verge of fainting. Though you want and desire to, you can hardly look at him or her or even mumble a "hello." Do you have this kind of feeling towards someone? If so, you are seriously crushing it!

Unexpected Love

Although it's not the best kind of love to feel, unrequited love might be your first romantic experience. One-sided love that is unrequited is frequently heartbreaking. It occurs when you have feelings for someone but are aware that they may not feel the same way about you and may never like you back, despite your hopes that they will—you may have even tried a few "love spells" and charms.

The strange thing about this kind of love is that, despite your deep knowledge that you can never be happy in this relationship, you find yourself falling more and more in love with the person every day. You cheer on their victories, mourn their defeats, and show them your affection from afar. Even though it breaks your heart, you have to love that person.

It's this kind of affection that would make you believe that love is something negative. Nevertheless, you will learn the worth and beauty of reciprocal love through this kind of love.

Infatuation with Love

This appears to be lovely, but if unchecked, it might be dangerous. When you are infatuated with someone, you feel alone and powerless without them. If you have dealt with unrequited love in the past, you are more likely to encounter this kind of love for the first time.

Fear, insecurity, and possessiveness are common characteristics of obsessive love. Whether or not they are in a relationship, an insecure lover is infatuated with the other person and will do whatever to spend as much time as possible with them. When you love someone really, you feel afraid of losing them. You may also come to the realization that they are tired of you and just want to go away from you since you have been too available to them.

This kind of love isn't the best kind. When your love interest or partner goes, it will probably end in heartbreak because your "omnipresence" and insecurities robbed love from your life. There is no happy ending to this kind of relationship, so get treatment if you're in it.

lustful affection

Some of our crushes typically experience this kind of love (it starts in the imagination). We are all too familiar with this sensation: you see someone and instantly become attracted to them.

An embrace from that person sends the well-known "shiver" down your spine and gives you the impression that your body and soul are being shocked by an electrical charge.

Lusty love is the kind of love you feel for someone you are strongly (and usually hopelessly) attracted to sexually. When you're in this kind of love, all you can think about is getting close to that special someone—either to kiss, hug, or even simply touch them.

You are in passionate love if all you can think about while you are in love is getting to know and experience someone physically.

Self-centered Love

Love of this kind can be terrible, yet it's considered intelligent. It concerns two individuals who share romantic feelings for one another. It occurs when you fall in love with someone, but that person doesn't love you back because they are more in love with themselves. It's a narcissistic form of affection.

Typically, the person you love or vice versa will enter into a relationship with you purely out of curiosity; they have no genuine interest in you or your well-being. One individual desires love but is unwilling to return it when it comes to selfish love, which is one-sided. For self-serving purposes, all he or she wants is to see what they may gain from the relationship. This is the essence of self-centered love: It is poisonous.

Amorous Love

The most beautiful sort of love is romantic love. It is brimming with happiness, butterflies, rainbows, and sultry love tunes that seem to be speaking to you. The world appears to be an extremely wonderful place because of your love interest. Your tummy tingles at the mere mention of him or her, as if little butterflies were fluttering within.

You instantly smile, and your face brightens at the mention of his or her name. You both want this love and can't help but want to be with this person all the time since you love them, and they love you back.

You have discovered one of the most exquisite forms of love if this is how you are feeling. The world grins back to you because you are happy and smiling at it. This is the epitome of romantic love that you are feeling.

Love Without Conditions

The most unique kind of love is this one. If you are fortunate enough to experience it, it is truly a blessing and a miracle. The nature of unconditional love serves as an inspiration for most romantic plays, films, and books.

When someone loves you unconditionally, you care about them

more than anything else in the world and love them more than you love yourself. You are experiencing a unique kind of love that some people never have in their lives if you love and care for someone else with such selflessness.

This kind of love requires a great deal of faith, both in your own ability to handle the good and the bad in your romantic partner and in the ability of your special someone to return the favor. It needs communication, hope, trust, and even more love to achieve the latter.

Can you identify which of the above-discussed types of love you are experiencing? Do you truly want to use it to define your love life, and is it healthy for you? (All of your subsequent relationships are shaped by the first love you had). I hope you are content with the kind of love you have. In the following chapter, we'll talk about how to live it and make it extraordinary.

The initial kiss

Congratulations! Your love interest has noticed you and seems to like you back! Next, what are you going to do? I take it that you'll go on the first date? The first kiss moment is something that young love, especially romantic love and a crush, looks forward to more than the first embrace or handshake. The majority of young couples frequently worry about what to expect from their first intimate moment as they gaze at each other's lips.

Why Does the First Kiss Matter So Much? Your new relationship will succeed or fail based on that first kiss. It might spark more wonderful kisses or put an end to a developing romance. What should you do if your heart is pounding with anxiety and anticipation, leaving you feeling disoriented and disoriented (because you have no idea how your date will react)?

It's important to nail the first kiss since it's similar to the glue that holds a relationship together. You need to cement the relationship properly if you want it. You never know what's going to happen; it's like diving into enigmatic, black waters.

Even if you are the most confident kisser in the world, you could become a nervous wreck the first time you kiss someone you really care about. However, you can enter these enigmatic, murky waters and change the odds to your advantage.

Let's talk about how to make your first kiss unforgettable and wonderful.

How To Have The Perfect And Most Memorable First Kiss

You shouldn't be too concerned with the outcome because trying to do so is a surefire way to fail. Take your time and be cautious.

Arrange

It might appear to be an unforeseen incident that happens in the heat of the moment, as seen in the films. But in reality, it doesn't happen "out of the blue"; rather, the environment you two establish around one another comes first.

After spending a good amount of time together, it's ideal to kiss each other. This allows you some time to get to know one another better. Furthermore, you ought to be by yourself; nobody ought to be watching or interjecting. You must prepare if you want such an environment.

Make plans to go on a date or go somewhere where you will spend more time together in a setting that encourages bonding, such as a quiet restaurant, a movie theatre, or even just watching a movie at home. Ensure that you have some alone time at the end of the date; this could be spent in a car or on a deserted park seat.

Boost the libido

Do you worry that your partner might not want to return the kiss? As the evening goes on, create sexual tension if you want to make sure he or she does. You ask, "How can I do that?" The ideal non-intrusive technique to share some of your sexual vibes with your partner is to sit close to them.

Second, be mindful of your pitch and tone. Use a gentle, low voice when speaking; it will be calming and charming. It's an organic turn-on. Tell your lover how much you value and affirm them when you speak. You might compliment him or her on how gorgeous they are and how good it makes you feel to be with them. After the date, discuss how fantastic the date is or was. A kiss becomes enticing as a result of these behaviors, which intensify intimacy and sexual tension. Your lover will want to kiss you back because you started the process when you selected the ideal location.

Be Aware of Your Position

Where you kiss tells a lot about you. You're apprehensive enough about having to kiss your date for the first time; you don't want to add to your anxiety by worrying about who could be watching or about something unexpected that could ruin the moment. You must, therefore, use caution while choosing the venue where it will take place.

If you're scared that her mother could answer the door and catch you in the act, it's preferable to kiss in a parking lot rather than in front of her house (this worry can cause you to be clumsy instead of being the good kisser you know you are).

Steer clear of distractions.

A first kiss moment might be ruined by a plethora of factors besides humans. You may lose your love interest if that ideal moment is destroyed because you can never get it back. The sound of a cell phone ringing, a full bladder, chewing gum, an unfocused mind, and so forth are examples of distractions. Put an end to your mind's constant chatter and, if at all possible, ensure that your date is just thinking about this special moment with you.

Personal cleanliness

Are you tidy? Do you have a pleasant scent? Poor personal hygiene is repulsive. Imagine being kissed by someone who stank of sweat or had foul breath. What would you think about that? It goes without saying that you would not want to kiss them back or even come near their mouth.

A deodorant could be used to mask the stench of perspiration. A breath mint could be useful if you have dinner that includes garlic and your breath isn't the best. Moreover, swallow some water shortly before kissing to make your lips more moisturizing and kissable. This will make the kiss easier and slightly hotter.

Use the Appropriate Touch to Send the Signal

When trying to get cozy with your new "flame," pay attention to how you touch them since it sets the stage for the ideal kiss. You could play with his or her fingers or touch their arm or shoulder all the time. Keep in mind that you should playfully and softly approach your date in a way that both of you find comfortable.

You might say anything as simple as "you smell nice" or "I love your smile" to him or her as you get closer to the "kiss moment." There's no better way to say "I want to kiss you" than to mess with his or her hair (this works best for girls).

Never Think Your Partner Can Read Your Mind!

Even though you've followed all the advice and taken all the required actions, your date doesn't seem to get that you want to kiss them. When your date is unable to read your thoughts and react appropriately, what should you do?

Take it on! It is not necessary to force a kiss because of this. Tell your date that you would like to kiss them as clearly as you can. As you get closer to their face, wait for them to approach you more closely. Look for alternative strategies to improve the chemistry if he or she doesn't.

For example, approach your date and plant your palm on their cheek. Gently press your lips to the side of his or her mouth, then see how they respond. Your partner is ready for a kiss if he or she shuts his or her eyes to the feeling. This is your cue to initiate the kiss!

However, if your date isn't making any indication that they'd like to kiss you, too, don't respond in an approachable manner. Instead, show patience and allow them more time. You have two options: either give up and find a nice diversion to mask your disappointment, or quit being needy and try again later.

Go Slowly

You shouldn't become irrationally agitated just because your date gave you permission to kiss them and even returned the favor. Take your time and observe how your date kisses; it might not be the same as your own. When their lips meet yours, pay close attention to how they feel. It may take a while to determine who is touching your upper or lower lip. Aggressive kissing might cause confusion as you try to integrate your techniques; even a small amount of uncertainty can ruin the mood.

My initial kiss

In the past, when he was my age, my father did not know anything, but thanks to the internet, I do now. It is simple to locate content, even poor-quality content.

When I watched the video that my friend had shared when I was a freshman, I was both shocked and ecstatic. I called it too late because my friend knew about this shit before me, and it's porn. I masturbated for several days while my mind recreated the events in the video. When it happened to me for the first time, I was astounded by what was happening to me and felt extremely happy for a brief while. I know this is bad and that I am making sin feel bad, but who knows? Maybe in a few months, it will become second nature, and I will enjoy feeling good while doing this.

Since Google is a well-known company worldwide and pays a lot of money, I have always wanted to work there. Google is all-knowing.
I want to have sex after watching porn, but it's difficult to find a partner in India, so I just masturbate. I detest this discussion, but what I do is watch porn without any sexual content; it's like a 1950s black-and-white film.

My teenager stays up late at school, and since I'm an introverted boy, I avoid talking to girls. I didn't make any girlfriends there, but I do like this one girl who, in my opinion, is really intelligent. Her reddish-brown hair and brown eyes make me smile every time I see her. Despite sitting next to each other during exams, we never had the confidence to approach her. My first love was, I believe, one-sided. She hasn't accepted me as a friend on Instagram yet.

Feelings, as you know, change with time. At that point, I wanted to become a doctor because all of my relatives were trying to become doctors but failed. My willpower was weak, so I took a year or so to consider what was best for me and decided to become a corporate lawyer. Since then, I've come to terms with my preferences and the areas where I can be creative without getting bored. I haven't failed yet, and I'm getting better at it, thank God.

We've struggled with money as a family since we were young. While Americans are free to live as they please, in our situation, we are insecure, kill our dreams and feelings, and do things that allow us to make money so that we can afford to live better lives. But because my brother has supported me up to this point, I was able to keep my dream alive. Apart from that, I still don't have a partner, and I'd like to have sex with someone. I would love it if my girlfriend were older than I am. I was not as experienced as she was. Since I'm an introvert, I should consider myself blessed if she's an extrovert. However, in reality, it hardly ever happens if she is lovely, sophisticated, and elegant. I fear that I loved her, and I would do anything for love.

This brings us to our main point. I created a profile on Bumble and Tinder yesterday. They both charge too much, but I did it in the hopes of finding a girlfriend. I'll be extremely fortunate if I get that, but who knows? I decided to catch up in the quiet bar today with a girl I know who is five years older than me because we had a good chat on chat yesterday, and I swiped through some of her profiles and chatted with her. A place where we can discuss and assess our suitability for friendship and a relationship. In today's modern India, I believe you can purchase happiness on a large scale if you have a sizable income. There are many things that money can buy, including time. Automobile, bus, train, plane, and hyperloop: You can get away from the time when you travel.

She was waiting for me outside the bar, looking through his phone, when I first saw her. She notices me as I approach her, and I notice that her jacket is attractive.

Hi, Jyoti. I apologize for being stuck in traffic; you are aware of the bit here.

She gave me an emotionless look and said, "I hate men when they are late."

Then she opened the bar's door and entered.

She appears to be berating me.

When I told her that I was only six minutes late and she was upset with me, I was really perplexed. I feel nervous because this is my first date in life, and I fucked it, I think.

We took the window seat and sat opposite each other. She is scrolling her phone again and typing something on it. I just sat there, looked at her with a smile, and thought about how I had started the conversation. What I say is, is she evaluating me or just doing time pass? Negative thoughts suppressing my mind then, I took a hard breath and said can we talk.

She said; hmm, what's your real name.

Jay

Why did you write the wrong name in your profile, Jay

Just do not want to share data with Tinder.

Ohh you think you are smart or over-smart

I am just an average who fears talking to a girl. (oh shit, what I said inflow)

She smiled and said to the waiter a bottle of champagne, please.

Jay, are you playing dumb? You talk to me in chat and now are talking about why you feel you are average. Are you still a virgin?

I just looked at her. Do you want to know how I feel?

Yes, sure, I want to know how much you are average.

Everyone has some emotion or thought word that I want to share with her, but I am not good at making friends; from childhood till now, I envy those people who can make friends and talk to anybody fearlessly. I am an introvert trying hard to become an extrovert. My father is an extrovert, and my brother is better at conversation than me. I feel jealous sometimes. This is a small achievement I do not have; I am trying to, but I do not know what I do when home; I feel lonely. There are plenty of numbers on my phone, but I am not able to talk to anybody. I feel pathetic watching movies and Netflix to kill loneliness. So, I am talking to you, Jyoti.

Are you feeling good when you see your life is better than mine?

Are you feeling better? She said you were smiling outside the bar when you were looking at me, and now you were a lonely boy. No one is talking to you. I am talking to you, Jay. If you feel comfortable, you can share your thoughts with me, and I think we can become a friend now as I know you better than before if you feel okay (I felt happy inside my heart when she told me this word to me. And she was smiling like she was breaking my heart. When you first attract a girl, you feel a special attraction like a magnet. You know, while looking into her eyes, if she is interested in you or not. Also, lips are a good sign for a kiss if her eyes are looking at your lips) Yeah, hmm, and cheer with our glass of wine.

Ya, I am sure you are a smart, handsome introvert and talk like an extrovert.

Oh, thanks. Sometimes, if I feel comfortable with the person whom I am talking to.

What if I cheated on you? What will you do

She asked me, and I just did not know what to reply.

I do not know what I would do if you cheated on me; I just do not know how I would react when I felt cheated.

She called the waiter and paid the bill, and also she gave her tips.

We watched some dancing in the Centre of the bar. She felt awakened, so we went out to the bar, where I searched for a cab on my phone, and she said to walk with me.

I looked at her, and she gave me a sign to come here, where she had parked her car. She came near to me; I dropped you what is your location. Can you drive a car?

I do not know how to drive. She looked at me and said I will teach you; next time, be ready.

She came near my place; she lived 5 km away from here. She looked at me. She looked at my lip.

We were just attracted to each other. She kissed me on my lip one time (my heartbeat was accelerating). I pulled her shirt towards my lip and kissed her. Lips over her lips, I feel energetic, and how can I tell you if you do not really kiss a girl in life before marriage? We kissed each other for 5 minutes, all her lipstick on my face, and she cleaned my face with a tissue. I want to have sex. She just held my hand open the car door and said, can we go upstairs? She parked the car, and we both held each other's hands together. We went to the lift, not kissing there because of CCTV.

When she came to my house, she opened the button on the shirt, and I opened her shirt. I just tore two of her shirt buttons. I ran out of time. We go to the bedroom, where she opens her hair. When I see her back with long hair and some tattoos on her waist, it looks like I am fully controlled by her beauty. We both are now naked. I am inexperienced; I do not know how to have sex. My heartbeat and breath are double, and I like only kissing her neck and pressing her boobs. It's in good shape, and she liked doing that; with her help, when my things go inside her after one minute of trying, I feel like going into a heated place. After some seconds, I cum inside her, and she was like do it again. (I feel nervous. What if I am pregnant with her) I was satisfied, but she was not. After some time, I again cum in 1 min. I was really trying to hold, but I'm sorry...

I just lost my virginity while she said to me come beside me; you lost too much energy. Tomorrow eats an apple.

I said I want to kiss tomorrow. You can get it now. Why wait? She comes near to me and kisses me, and in winter, we sleep beside each other naked. The whole night feels heated. This is my time experience of sleeping with someone naked.
The next day, she woke up early from me, and she, wearing my dress, looked like she was me. I smiled at her, and she said good morning.

I make good tea for her. She is taking an interest in my hobby, my work, and what I am doing. When I got out downstairs, she kissed my lip and face while she went to her car I was. Feeling sad somehow.Emotionally attached to her.

In the lift, one laughed at me when I saw him. After some time, I looked at my mirror. Her velvet lipstick was printed on my face. And you know in the morning we had sex again, that was really awesome in the morning, she said she would come next weekend.

It was the first time I felt sex was more awesome than masturbation. But again, I masturbate because she is not my wife whenever I want, wherever I want to have sex with her.

Last time, I told Jyoti I had a dream of having sex in a car. Can we do it next time? She told me I also wanted to but did not know if someone saw us create a new problem. I know the place downstairs in the parking. Next time, we can smile at me, kiss me, and say your fantasies too much.

But again, we are girlfriend and boyfriend now, and we have sex in weekends and sometimes every day. My new addiction is sex. Without it, I feel sad. And Doggystyle and in the kitchen is my favorite shit with my love Jyoti. Fantasy about sex is making me crazy sometimes; I feel I am raping her. But she never told me to stop. I do not want this; you are bad like that.

When with her shirt, I tied her hand on my back doing anal morning sex with her whenever I felt frustrated with my job. Sometimes, I blind her eyes and bind her hand with broad tape and do blowjobs. She is very good at it.

She satisfied me with her blowjob. Now we live together. Whenever we go out in the car, she gives me a blowjob downstairs. She is loyal to me, and I am loyal to her.

And one day, when driving a car, she crashed into a truck on the highway. I spotted death on the road when I was in the office and got a call on my phone; I took it and was totally shocked. While investigating, they found out she was fully drunk, and it was her fault. Looks like suicide, and the police interrogated me, but they did not find out the exact reason for her death because of lack of evidence. I watched Dexter, so it's not easy for Indian police to accuse me. Also, I am a lawyer, so they closed that investigation. I know as she died because of me, I was just broken, not knowing where I would make mistakes for what I did to her. I know after her death, she was pregnant, and she did not want me to become a father because I was only hungry for sex, I think.

She wrote an encrypted email, which I got after her death, where she said she feared me. Sometimes, she wanted to kill me, but she also loved me because (I was the devil in bed; I was good from the outside and never offended her or abused her, always did what she asked for). I treated her like a dog doing blowjobs every day. Her neck was swallowed. She felt devastated; she was fired from the company because of me. She was feeling depressed like me when I was lonely and wanted her to become my friend, not money in a bank account. She is living with me but never told me any of this stuff. I think she does not trust me now. One day, when she found out she was pregnant, she wanted to talk to me, and she thought like having the last hope to live, but that day, I did stuff very much with her. She was crying after that, and the next morning she died.

After reading that email, I cried for her because, in the last line, she said Jay, I love you; you are also my first love, Jay. You respect me but not my body; next time, girl, no, don't do that, Jay. You break my heart so much. After that, I just felt broken; I know now I never loved her; I only wanted his body for sex; after that incident, I went into mental depression for some time, went to my parent's house, and lived there for some time, but in memory, she comes to every day with blood in her hand looking at me sometimes in a dream that is my sin that I got from God.

Every year, we worship for her and for her soul. Do not have sex after that.

Every day, I regret why I do that. Why am I like this? I am just trying to live without her because, after her death, I feel very lonely. No one is talking to me like earlier when I first saw her in an outside silent bar looking at me. Her kiss, her dress, it comes in my dream. Sometimes, I also wanted to die but never got so much courage as Jyoti. I missed her, and my life become shit now because of the wrong decision I took in my life for my self-interest.

With the sun beaming down on the busy downtown streets, it was a stunning early spring day. Two strangers were going down the same busy pavement in opposing directions amid the throngs of people racing to and fro. They were too preoccupied with their own ideas and plans for the day to see one other at first. But there was a sense of promise and expectation in the air as they got closer. Everything changed when they finally laid eyes on one another.
It was the woman who saw him first; he was a tall man wearing a sharp suit, with his hair pulled back, and his eyes

focused intensely on his phone. Even though it was her first time seeing him, she had a sudden wave of recognition. She seems to have been waiting her entire life for this moment. The man raised his head in time to meet hers, and their eyes met for a brief instant. They couldn't understand the quick, intense connection that they felt.

As they walked on, their steps became more deliberate and deliberate, with each of them glancing back at the other. They didn't realize they would never know what may have happened if they had stopped to talk until they were no longer in sight. However, destiny had different intentions for them, ones that would reunite them in ways they could never have predicted.

Chapter 2: Transient Passion

Weeks passed, and the recollection of that accidental street meeting started to erode. Both the man and the woman continued living their lives, pursuing their hobbies and aspirations. However, there lingered in the background of their thoughts a sense of unresolved matters that neither of them could get rid of. They pondered whether the connection they'd felt was genuine or imagined, as well as what would have happened if they had taken the time to converse that day.

Then, one night, destiny got involved once more. The man felt a tap on his shoulder as he struck up a conversation with a few strangers at a networking event. The woman from the street was there waiting for him as he turned around, looking as beautiful as he recalled. A surge of emotion swept over him as she smiled at him. The fact that she was standing in front of him and that fate had once again brought them together astounded him.

They had a brief conversation in which they made small talk about the event and exchanged niceties. But as the night went on, he couldn't help but be pulled to her and want to learn more about her life. He had never felt more at ease and comfortable than he did in her company while they laughed and joked together. After years apart, they seemed to be old friends getting back together.

However, the woman had to depart as the night was coming to an end. The man, unable to put into words, felt a sense of loss and remorse as he watched her leave. He was aware that he needed to visit her once more in order to investigate the connection they had made at the event and on the street. Silently, he promised himself that he would do whatever it took to make it happen.

Chapter 3: A Retake

The man and the woman started going out more often after their accidental encounter at the networking event. They took long walks around the city, went out for coffee, and shared dinner. Their bond became stronger every time they spent time together because they had similar senses of humor, shared interests, and growing comprehension of each other's aspirations.

"I feel like I've known you forever," the man said to the woman as they strolled hand in hand along the riverbank one evening. We seem to have been destined to meet."

The woman grinned, and her eyes brightened with comprehension. "I understand your point," she remarked. "It's like we've been waiting for each other all our lives."

Walking on, they relished the pleasant breeze and the sound of the waves crashing onto the coast. The man turned to face the woman as the sun was lowering and stated, "I want to make the most of this moment together. I'd like to give us a try. Are you going to join me out? Correctly, that is. when out on a date."

With her heart pounding quickly, the woman glanced at him. "Yes," she responded without thinking twice. "I'd like that very much."

And thus, it came to pass that they went on their first official date—a wonderful evening that would determine the destiny of their relationship. They were both filled with excitement and anticipation as they sat across from one another in a small restaurant, sipping wine and exchanging stories. They were aware that they were setting off on a brand-new journey that would permanently alter their lives.

Chapter 4: Love at First Sight

Day by day, the man and the woman's feelings for one another intensified as they kept seeing one other. They learned new things about one another, and every new insight they gained strengthened their belief that their union was meant to be.

They explored the city and found new cafés and eateries while spending quiet days reading books and watching films. Together, they joked and laughed, and occasionally, they would discuss the future and all the adventures they could go on.

Even though they had a great time together, they were aware that their relationship extended deeper than just a simple attraction or interest in similar things. They were experiencing a sensation that both excited and alarmed them: falling in love.

"I don't want to be anywhere else but here with you," the woman murmured to the man as they lay in bed one night. You give me such a sense of life.

The man grasped her hand tightly. He answered, "I feel the same way." Before I met you, I had no idea what it felt like to be in love. However, I can no longer fathom my life without you."

Their hearts began to beat in unison as they fell in love. They were aware that there would be difficulties along the way and that their adventure together was only getting started. However, they were prepared to meet them head-on since they had faith that their love would be strong enough to withstand whatever life threw at them.

Chapter 5: The Initial Obstacle

The guy and the woman faced their first significant obstacle as their love became stronger. The man had to travel a lot for work, often for weeks at a time. The woman tried to be understanding at first, but as the days stretched into weeks, she realized how much she missed him. Nothing could take away the pain in her heart, no matter how hard she tried to divert her attention to her job and friends.

Sitting alone in her flat one night, the woman realized she couldn't carry on in this manner. Even though it might put their relationship in jeopardy, she realized she had to tell the man how she felt.

She requested him to meet her for coffee over the phone the next day. She inhaled deeply and remarked, "I know your job is important, and I don't want to stand in the way of your success," when he arrived. But I have to tell you the truth. It's difficult for me to be away from you for this long. I can't express how much I miss you."

The man gave her a look, understanding softening his gaze. "It's difficult," he said.

"I promise, I also miss you. However, I value my work and don't want to let it go."

With tears in her eyes, the woman nodded. "I recognize that," she murmured. However, I can't carry on feeling this way. Is there a chance we could work things out? Could I perhaps accompany you on some of your travels?"

With a hint of hope in his eyes, the man grinned. He answered, "I'd love that." "In case it was too much for you, I was hesitant to recommend it. However, I think it could be fantastic if you're willing. As a team, we could explore new places and traverse the world."

And so, in spite of the difficulties that would lie ahead, they made the decision to begin their lives together. They were prepared to attempt even though they knew it wouldn't be simple since their love was worth fighting for.

I immediately forcefully inhale a massive amount of breath as soon as he moves away from the desk. Emerson Jacks is not one of those absurdly broad-shouldered guys who, when they have a break from hurling buildings around, grunt and groan and deadlift two hundred pounds. Nope. His build is perfect. There are muscles visible beneath the light pink T-shirt, but you can still feel them there. I've seen those muscles contract as he's leaned his hand against a desk and made a valiant effort to control my heart rate.

Yes. The guy just stands there and gets to me. He looks fantastic. His hair is a deep brown color, with a chunk that falls across his forehead. Bluish eyes.Kind gaze.

But I'm sure of his strength. He once helped Abbie Arbour when she passed out in the hallway, and I saw it. Abbie is amazing; she resembles Rebel Wilson before the actress was underweight. I respect Abbie because she doesn't think diet nonsense should ruin her high self-esteem. She should be a clear conviction to all of us. I'm not. When I am not cramming to finally make something of myself, I worry about how I appear and the extra weight. The Adams family's first college graduate. It's a difficult burden to carry, but not because of other people or my wonderful family.

Because of me, I'm fully committed. I really want to be here. I adore this location.

Nevertheless, Em lifted her up as if she were a feather—not quite, but almost—and carried her to the nurse's office. He did not strain. He held her with enough ease to be insanely gentle.

My memory of that moment is still burnt. She received kindness from the intensely focused man who seemed to be making a big difference in his life. When she needed someone, he was there for her.

He was the same earlier this semester when we worked on a project together under Prof. Hawthorne's guidance. Working together for almost two weeks was an absolute blast. Em is perceptive and has an unmatched ability to focus on details. However, he found my jokes funny and laughed heartily. However, he was kind to me when I shut down or became grumpy—yes, I know it's my M.O., and it's not pretty. I kept reading his eyes, and there seemed to be something there. For myself.

Perhaps I was just dreaming?

The professor then divided our group when a new student arrived late for class. He introduced me to an established pair and paired Em with the new child. However, in our brief time together, I came to realize one thing.

There's something exceptional about that guy. Something he has that I want.

Furthermore, I'm aware that I'll never have it.

However, the student in front of me is waiting. April Harris is here, and she gives me her slip. Her anxious expression strikes me—she's got a deadline. I rush to comfort her. "Let me check to see if this was given back."

I smile at April, who already has a huge stack of books in her arms. Similar to her. If she could, she would take the entire library home. However, I enjoy her. I open the book because I want to help. It's no longer in.

I'm not done yet, though. I check the time on my spiral notebook and wonder if Dax Williams, TA (Theatre Arts) 411, who has been eating it for the past few hours, would feel like eating soon. This person has been here for a long time and is a popular theatre student. If I ask, maybe he'll give up the book now so April can have it for the little time it has left.

Jenny, a fellow student employed through the college work-study program, frequently chastises me for devoting more time and effort to the task at hand. Instead, she just says, "Try later!" with joy and moves on to the next pupil. I am the only one who has experienced not receiving the assistance required when needed. Not everyone is blessed with a lifetime of possibilities.

I informed April that I'll speak with Dax in private to find out if he's still using it. He's well over to the right by the enormous Christmas tree, which is adorned with strings of small, hand-made books that Thackeray students have made throughout the years. Adorable. She nods to the next student in the queue, and I ask her to wait.

"Two back in time. Hold on tight. I get up and start my quest. But Emerson Jacks keeps coming back to me. I am powerless to stop myself. He's studying right over there, nearby. With his head bent over the book, he is breathing in antiquities as if they were his last breath. I think about it again.

I wanted to switch places with someone more than just the one time I saw him with Abbie. Not the first time I'd wished he was staying, as I gawked at that trim ass in dark jeans as he left my territory alongside me.

The reality makes my stomach turn. He has a certain grounded quality. Sexiness is merely a plus. Before I can stop myself, I sigh.

Desire.

Simply want.

However, even if there had been a probability of such in the past, it vanished now. With time running out, the only daughter in the illustrious Adams family, who is expected to get a highly sought-after dual degree in both antiquities and ancient languages, has to face a

Christmas present she truly wishes she could return to life.

As early as tomorrow morning, I was on my way home, my aspirations of earning a degree dashed.

Two Emerson

I'm seated at my table, delving deeply into the ancient Greek antiquities book that's in front of me.

Eli Austin, from Delta North Security Force, a new company I'm enthusiastic about working with, sent me a text message that was full of stuff I should read. He will oversee I.T. for my cousin's team; therefore, I need to make an impression on him if I want to get the position there. This book is plastered to my ass since it's on his list.

He's also extremely qualified to lead me, having been one of Cole's special operations comrades.

My desire to be a part of this new endeavor is screaming through my veins once more. A security company run by the former commander of a fucking elite combat unit? I totally agree. It also appears that my cousin is rather famous, even though, to me, he has always just been Cole Dawson.

Cole is a decent man. Yes, he's all business with me at the moment, but I understand. I have to establish my worth. I have to prove to him that I am capable of handling the guys on the team—military men—and that he won't have to watch after me just because I'm family. These men, who hail from various parts of the nation, were all part of Cole's Delta North Team Special Ops team in Afghanistan.

They are currently organizing the security company and figuring out the logistics. Being a community guy and the leader of the family ranch, Cole appreciates the assistance. He monitors everyone in the Dawson Ridges area to make sure they're all okay. The man is really busy despite the fact that his wife Tabby fully participates in everything; the family and ranch workers try their best to assist him. Whether related or not, they truly are a family there on the ranch. It's a pleasant area to be in. I should know; my brothers, Wes and Connor, and I grew up there extensively.

I scan the room, taking in every child in the soft light that fills the library. They're just getting started, just like me.

However, I have a chance that none of them will. I'm incredibly fortunate. I won't let it slip away.

And it's not just Cole. His squad consists of guys that I've met. They have all experienced many hardships, including war. Special operations. Unquestionably well beyond my pay grade.

However, the opportunity to begin working with such individuals, who are really knowledgeable and are creating something significant, is unbeatable. This is an opportunity of a lifetime. I don't consider myself to be a corporate type, and I have no intention of doing grocery shopping or petrol pumping.

But handling security cases for individual citizens? Recovering artwork and antiquities? Yes, that's right. There's still more. Cole approved my participation in one of their planning calls, and they will also be accepting situations involving missing persons. Kidnappings and contracts for bodyguards. We're back to the entire art and antiquities thing, so they'll be watching stuff. They'll also perform extractions.

Thus, I hadn't left Cole in the dark about the new endeavor when I learned about it over the grapevine at a family gathering.

As expected, he drew me aside and gave me a hard lecture about work ethic, contribution, and principles. After that, he instructed me not to bother him for a year and firmly handed me off to the other guys on the squad.

He was not going to watch over me or hold my hand. If I was sincere, he expected me to step up and make my own contribution. As soon as the guys got to know me, I could tell he would see how everything worked out. Hell, it flung me into the wind without even providing a rudder. I'm a competent shipwright. The opportunity to truly show who I am makes me happy.

In summary? I had lived, breathed, eaten, and slept in Delta North ever since I learned about it. That force has to include me. I had to participate in it.

Which brought me to Thackeray and my current major.

This year is ill. The professors are excellent, and the studies are in-depth. In addition, I'm making acquaintances in the Maine small town where Thackeray College, commonly referred to as T.C., is situated. I'm confident that my network of associates will be helpful no matter where I work.

The best part is that I'm learning enough background information to really help Delta North. Convince them to hire me on the basis of my qualifications rather than just the fact that we are related.

I thumb through the thick book, looking for the part I need to memorize. Greek antiquities. Currently in-demand pieces; I am not sure where they are. I ignore the fading Deck the Halls carol that is playing as I fix my gaze on a precious cup, quickly scanning the description and storing it away in my memory. Despite the significant portion of my heart that a certain girl holds, I'm determined to succeed. Something I will do my best to handle.

I hunch down to study.

A few minutes later, a scuffle at the reference desk breaks my concentration. I glance in that direction and scowl, and I'm not alone. The brunette from the adjacent table meets my gaze and shakes her head; students are winking all around me. Two of the naughtiest boys in the university, Colin and Darian, are slouching over the desk far too near to Callie. Even though it's all fake bravado, the lady generally has the upper hand, but this evening, something about the way she looks bothers me. Her body language is protective, and she has retreated significantly.

The glimmer of terror in those violet eyes is something I detest.

Colin whispers to Callie, "I'll have it back in the morning, baby," his voice is clear above the abrupt silence in the space. Those two are really big jerks. As long as they achieve their goals, they don't care who they offend or what they do.

Not at all. Overnights. Callie highlights. Her remarks reverberate across the room, and it's clear that they're not her first.

B*tch. Does she have a tremor in her lower lip?

Darian bends over the desk, sits on its edge, and runs a finger down the center of the book she's been reading. Gradually.Laboriously. It's harsh and sickly suggestive for what it is—just a finger and a book. He holds her eyes and fixes his eerie look on her.

"Because you did the favour, baby, we can give you extra time." I can still hear his voice even if he is lowering it. I have remarkable hearing, which is both a blessing and a problem. "Have you ever doubled?"

I yank back my chair. Everyone looks at me when I screech. Not important. Callie, or any other woman, for that matter, won't be harassed by them. Not with me here. At all.

But my heart is drained. The faculty member in charge of the library, Ms. Thornberry, emerges as though out of nowhere. Most of us who are close to retirement and articulate know better than to urinate in her Cheerios.

Cassie sees a tall, sturdy, grey-haired figure at the desk, and as she gets closer, both of the goons step out of her personal space at once.

Colin muses, "Uh, hello, Mizz Thornberry." "I was merely..."

"Guys, it's closing time."

She gives them a smile that only she can give—the one with the steel trap hidden beneath it. She turned to face the room and made her statement, brushing them off as insignificant as crumbs on the carpet.

All of you, gather your belongings. Right now. She delicately places her palm on Whitman's desk edge as though they were still the closest of friends from a bygone period. It seemed as though she could rely on him to arrive and slap some wealthy people without any concern. She slips her vintage silver charm bracelet on her wrist. "Talk to you in a week. Go now!

Everyone understands. However, I don't like how irate those two idiots are looking.

First Chapter: Catalyst

Evan didn't bother to lock the flat after leaving, instead slamming the door shut and running out. From his second-floor landing, he bounded down the stairs, using the guardrail for stability, jumping the last half and racing towards his locked bicycle.

Oh no! Why had today been the day of all the days to wake up late? As he rapidly released his bike, he thought to himself and slung his leg over the saddle, pedaling as quickly as he could.

He was out of the apartment block and speeding by the corner convenience shop in less than a minute. Upon glancing at his father's ancient watch, he realized he had a mere fifteen minutes to reach school or risk missing the English exam that morning.

Even though he was only four weeks into his high school career, he was taking his second significant test of the year today. One of the strictest instructors on campus, Mr. Hanson, was his English teacher. He would lock him out of class if he was late, which would have further impacted his already precarious GPA. Had it not been for a phone call he received moments ago from his pals Oliver and Katie, he would still be slept soundly at home, thus jeopardizing his chances of getting into college.

He looked at his watch once more as he turned the final bend leading to the school, and the hands read 8:08.

With a ragged breath, he snarled, "Shit!"

Even though he was having trouble recalling everything he had packed into his head, he couldn't help but laugh at the absurdity of the situation—that he had studied late the night before for this same test.

For a moment, his mind wandered to the outcomes of his first exam, which had been two weeks earlier. He had originally received a respectable 81%, but his penmanship had cost him two points, bringing his final score down to 79%. A less than inspiring message reading "You can do better than this" had been scribbled across the top in bright red ink, compounding the injury.

Ignoring his aching muscles and the increasing ache in his side, Evan pumped his legs as hard as he could. When he heard the early bell sound, he briefly experienced a glimmer of hope that he may make it to the school, which was now finally within sight. He had five minutes to go to class once the bell rang.

After lowering his head and exerting even more effort, Evan arrived on campus in a matter of minutes. He leaped off his bike and ran into class with an athleticism befitting a desperate man, shrieking with fear at the sound of metal hitting metal as his bike crashed into the chain-link fence at the rear.

He didn't dare slow down as he dashed around the final bend to his English lesson, taking it at full speed and leaning in heavily to keep as much momentum as possible. And then, WHACK!

He struck something hard and felt a numbing sensation creep across his chest and down his left arm. Pain flared across his shoulder.

He felt disoriented and dazed as he staggered, not understanding quite what had happened. He still had time to make it to class; that much was evident. He scrambled desperately, straightened, and dashed off.

Evan looked over his shoulder to see what he had struck as he went. For an instant, he saw a girl, her hair shining silver, lying on the ground with her long dark skirt flung down to her knees.

"I apologise," he yelled over his shoulder as he dashed towards his English class's door, which was now in view.

The numbness subsided as he ran the final few steps, bringing with it a searing ache that helped clear his confused thoughts. As the agony worsened, he hated himself for not stopping to make sure she was okay following such a violent collision

And felt guilty for not checking on her. But time was just not on our side.

Evan arrived as the bell indicating the start of class rang, and he threw his foot inside the doorway just before the teacher closed it.

Mr. Hanson panted fiercely, sweat streaming off of him, and he stared at Evan.

The teacher responded, "You're late, Mr. Morgan," and then slightly opened the door to let Evan in.

Evan slithered in, relief coursing through him as he moved to his desk and collapsed into his seat a moment later. "Thank you, sir," he whispered.

Oliver grinned softly, "That was close," while Evan wiped the perspiration from his brow and ran his fingers through his light-brown hair.

Mr. Hanson went to his desk on the far side of the room, where a little stack of test packets was lying, and locked the door.

"Now that Mr. Morgan's grand entrance is over, let's get started," he murmured. "Clear your desks, everyone. Could you please give these out, Miss Lopez? The brunette was seated right in front of the teacher's desk as he handed out the packets to her.

Katie cast a furtive look at Evan through her spectacles as Maria started passing out test stacks to each row.

After moving to the town in the middle of his third grade, Evan made his first friends in Riverview in elementary school, where he eventually met Katie. Her large round glasses and long, braided chestnut hair from that era remained in his memory. Despite the fact that she had cut her hair much shorter in their freshman year, they had become fast friends and stayed close ever since. Evan cherished her intelligent, compassionate nature as well as the bursts of intense anger that periodically erupted from him or Oliver—things they did to make her angry.

Katie shook her head, grimacing, and returned her focus to the upcoming test while Evan grinned back at her.

Evan's arm and chest surged in vivid pain as the last of the numbness left him. Wondering who he'd bumped into and why she was carrying a rucksack full of bricks, he glanced back at the door. Did she feel alright? Did she require assistance?

A sudden feeling of fear came over him as he heard a knock on the door. Had anyone seen what had transpired? Was he about to face consequences for hitting someone? Had she suffered a serious injury or worse?

Mr. Hanson sighed loudly as he crossed the room once more. Taking a quick look around, he was able to quickly identify the lone missing pupil.

He uttered the words loudly enough to be heard through the door, "You know the rules, Mr. Simmons." "On test day, you have to wait until the exam is finished if you arrive late. He stopped in the middle of his statement and yanked the door open. "You can make it up after—"

Evan was devastated to see a young lady with vivid silver hair and a dark skirt standing in place of the gaunt, blonde kid he had slammed with minutes before. All eyes in the class turned to her arrival and Mr. Hanson's astonished silence.

Mr. Hanson paused for a moment before gathering himself. Indeed? I'm in the midst of class," he declared sharply.

The girl gave him one of the crumpled pieces of paper from the jumbled pile in her hands without saying anything. Mr. Hanson paused for a second, then picked up the given paper and stepped back. Evan thought, despite the absurdity of the idea, that the teacher had been briefly startled by the girl's appearance as Mr. Hanson read.

Evan couldn't help but ogle her while she waited for Mr. Hanson to respond; she was, without a doubt, one of the most attractive girls he had ever seen. Her hair was unusually long, falling around her in a brilliant silver waterfall that reached well past her waist and swept behind her. She had lovely, round cheeks, steel-colored eyebrows, and light, creamy skin. Evan initially assumed the teacher had pale green eyes, but when she moved, he saw that the color was actually silver, reflecting the green of Mr. Hanson's shirt.

Maybe he was just feeling bad for earlier, but there was something enigmatic and fascinating about her that drew him in. That was beyond her unique appearance.

Even though he was positive they had never met, he couldn't shake the feeling that there was something strangely familiar about her.

Mr. Hanson moaned as he unlocked the door for the newcomer after reading for a while. "All right, Miss Blackmore, please enter. Turn your tests face down, everyone, and don't start until I tell you to.

As Mr. Hanson led the new student to the front of the class, the room stayed eerily silent.

"Everyone, take note!" Mr. Hanson spoke needlessly because all eyes were already fixed on the two of them. "A new student is enrolled in our class today. I expect everyone to assist her in settling in as she recently relocated to Riverview. Would you kindly introduce yourself, Miss Blackmore?

Evan noticed that the class seemed to be fascinated by the newcomer. He was bursting at the seams to find out who she was and why she had traveled to his little corner of the globe.

Though the atmosphere was oddly adversarial, a low level of whispering among the other students gradually increased, and he heard a few whispers that said, "What's wrong with her?" and "Why was she required to enroll in our class?" "He better not bring her back here," they said. The room was swept by a chilly breeze as though the cold reactions were now palpable.

He looked more closely to determine what might cause such instantaneous hostility because he couldn't grasp everyone's seeming disgust. He looked at her dazzling silver hair for a moment, then brushed it aside. Though it was certainly odd, individuals on campus frequently dyed their hair in colors other than natural ones. Many females and a few boys with vivid red, green, or blue hair were there. There was also no reason to disagree with her choice of attire. Autumn had arrived, and although it wasn't quite cold, her long-black skirt and blue turtleneck sweater matched those of many other students.

She was unusually pale, it was true, but not to the extent that it should worry everyone. She had a slightly ethereal appearance from her colorless eyes, which he believed would have intrigued other people more than alarmed them. Her skin tone, pale eyes, and silver hair created an unusually monochromatic look. For a moment, Evan pondered if her recent illness could account for her commencing classes four weeks into the semester.

He stared at mass craziness for a few moments, then gave up trying to figure out why everyone looked so eager to reject her.

The girl's hands were folded in front of her as the seconds passed still. Her head was lowered, avoiding all eye contact. The murmuring gradually became louder as another cold wave blew through the room, and she retreated a cautious half step. Something stirred, Evan sensed. He felt compelled to defend her, and he thought it would be stupid to throw himself in the way of the awkward, defenseless girl and the oddly menacing class.

"Calm down," Mr. Hanson snapped. With a gentle, motivating shove forward, he reached over to say, "Go ahead, Miss Blackmore."

She took a deep breath and then spoke gently to the students. Hana is my name, she uttered. Hana Blackmore. I hope that everyone gets along.

With a kid in the back yelling, "Yeah, right!" and a few hushed giggles, the atmosphere in the room grew gloomier.

"Enough of that!" Mr. Hanson said, eyes darting around to find the offender as Evan peered about.

The class fell silent right away, and Mr. Hanson gestured to an empty desk in front of the room after a brief period of time.

"You are free to occupy that seat, Miss Blackmore."

Evan was relieved to see his friend Katie lean over and softly introduce herself to the newcomer as she settled into the chair. He was happy that not every student in the class was biased towards Hana, and he was not taken aback when Katie was the first to smile at her. The whispering stopped as Mr. Hanson took multiple documents out of a desk drawer and placed them on Hana's desk, her back to the others.

This morning, we have an exam on the topics and importance of historical literature and foundational U.S.

documents. Throughout the lesson, you are welcome to sit and go over the material, he said. "Please be quiet during tests, and if you have any questions, don't ask them until the test is finished. I do not tolerate interruptions during tests."

After giving a nod, Hana took the syllabus and started to read.

Mr. Hanson announced they might start the test, and Evan switched his focus to it, relieved that the drama around Hana was now gone.

Evan felt upbeat as he completed the test since the answers came to him quickly and easily. He had over ten minutes remaining as the test came to a close, which gave him enough time to review his responses and revise anything that seemed too clumsy.

After a short while, Mr. Hanson raised his voice. "Okay, class, close your packets and put down your pencils."

With barely a few minutes remaining until the end of the period, the other students hurriedly grabbed their stuff, anticipating what lay ahead.

Mr. Hanson called the class back to order, saying, "I need a volunteer to show Miss Blackmore around school today before you leave."

Evan wasn't shocked when just one hand was raised, given the unfavorable response Hana had received before. He was taken aback by their response, but he determined he wasn't going to let this chance pass him by and held out his hand. He was still very sorry for bumping into her, and he was hoping Mr. Hanson would choose him so he could say sorry. Additionally, he would be able to demonstrate to her that not all of the students were stupid and that at least one person was happy she had come to Riverview.

The teacher went back to Katie, the first person to volunteer, and sent him a fleeting glance. "Miss Pascal, I understand you have Mrs. Roberts up next?"

"Yes, ma'am!" Katie stated with almost controllable excitement.

Alright. Could you kindly take Miss Blackmore on a tour?

"Yes, ma'am!" Katie smiled.

When the bell rang, the other students began to pack things and go for their next lesson, causing the classroom to explode with activity and commotion. With a sense of disappointment at having lost his opportunity to apologize, Evan stuffed his belongings into his rucksack and headed out of the classroom. Oliver followed him a minute later, and together, they made their way into history.

Since middle school, Oliver has been Evan's best friend. At the conclusion of the previous year, the two of them had plotted to enroll in nearly identical courses for the upcoming semester and had arranged to be seated next to each other in all of their morning classes.

"Why didn't you hold up your hand to introduce yourself to the new girl?" Evan enquired as they strolled. "A girl has the opportunity to get to know you, and you never want to blow the chance to make a good first impression."

"Well, she's not really my kind of person," Oliver sighed.

"I was unaware that you had a type. I've always believed that you were game if she was breathing and open to having sex.

"Sir, that offends me!" Oliver said, mockingly outraged. "My good man, I happen to have very specific tastes." He found humor in his own joke.

Oliver seemed uninterested, which surprised Evan, too, and he chuckled with his friend. Regarding girls, he'd never known them to disagree, and he couldn't understand why anyone wouldn't be enthralled with Hana Blackmore.

Evan wondered whether Hana would show up in any of his other classes as he took his seat at his history desk. Nevertheless, he was unhappy not to see her again and walked with Oliver to their normal lunch site behind the science building when lunchtime came around a few hours later. Oliver saw Evan's lowered spirits right away.

They sat down on their favorite tree's little patch of grass, and he said, "Hey, man, what's wrong?" "I should have brought lunch,"

In actuality, the answer is yes. I was too busy to grasp anything. The tightness in Evan's shoulder flared up and started hurting again as he collapsed onto the grass, stretching while resting on his back.

"I assumed." Oliver grinned as he shoved a little bag of carrot sticks and more than half of his tuna salad sandwich.

"Well, what took place this morning?" Oliver enquired. "We bided our time until Katie gave us a call."

"I dozed off while reviewing for today's test." Evan gave a yawn. "Normally, I would do that stuff at work, but last night, I had a lot on my plate, so I tried to study when I got home." I must have fallen asleep.

Is your supervisor still out of town? Oliver enquired.

"Yes, for an additional two weeks." With a grunt, Evan sat back up, balancing on his healthy elbow and nibbling on a little piece of sandwich. "So, Vicky and I are the only part-timers covering the bookstore. I've recently had to work a lot more hours than usual.

Oliver stated, "I don't know how you do it," while sucking on some tuna and mayonnaise. Taking care of your sister, going to school, and working at the bookshop. I understand why today is not going well for you.

I'll grant you that it's a lot of work. However, that's not my concern.

Oh, I see. What's going on?"

Before responding, Evan put down his sandwich and took a sip from his water bottle. Do you know the new English girl? Hana Blackmore?

"The eerie individual with silver hair?"

"She's not eerie, but she is."

"How about her?" Slyly, Oliver smiled. "Are you telling me you already have a crush on her?"

"No, that's not the case." "Listen, I ran into her this morning, right before Mr. Hanson let me in," stumbled Evan.

"Dude," murmured Oliver. "You saw the bell ringing, and you stopped to hit on a girl? Brave!

"No, you stupid person. I bumped into her rather literally. I gave her a complete knockdown. I suppose that explains her tardiness.

Oliver shook his head, saying, "Dick move." What made you do that?

It wasn't deliberate! She was waiting for me as I rounded the corner of Building H in my haste to get to the test in time! There was not even a moment to avoid anything!

Oliver said, "Uh-huh," as he took another bite.

There wasn't enough time for me to stop and offer assistance. Had I quit, I would not have survived.

Section Five

"I am not, am I?" As we crossed the street, Josh inquired.

"No, I don't think so. But that's some wonderful news—you know your soul mate too, so that's even better," I said haltingly, hoping Josh would believe me even though I knew I was lying.

"Yes, I guess," he said thoughtfully at the time. "I want to know who she is. Jamie owns Sharmayne, Fayte is far too young, Shadow is with Thorn, Marietta is too old, and Vanessa is only seventeen, so that left me with one thing to say about her.

"Cheeky, I'm only seventeen too!"

"Yes, but Vanessa is still a little child at heart, and her true love will have to be a very patient man—a man who is most definitely not going to be me." "Yeah, but you are a mature seventeen."

"Well, you should consider yourself fortunate that you are aware of yours and that it isn't Belial Di Aberlie, as I don't think he will ever be able to love me." I gave him a little rub on the palm of his hand and said, "I think you are much better off not knowing who or where your Soul mate is." Then we started walking down towards the house.

Josh opted to go for a jog in the park after we had one last kiss on the porch before heading inside. Ultimately, I believe he was just looking for some time to himself before confronting the others. I opened the door and nearly bumped into Belial, who was standing in the doorway of his office chatting to Thorn, our gazes meeting.

"Des, are you okay?" With a kind grin, Thorn questioned.

Desperate to get my eyes off Belial, I said to him, "Yes, I have homework to do. See you at dinner."

I was heading up the stairs to the second floor when I felt a hand grab me. I swung around to see Belial firmly grasping my wrist.

I attempted to back away, but he held on tightly.

"Destiny, I just want to talk." With pain in his voice, he said.

I yelled angrily, "Well, I don't so get your hands off me. You said enough last night to last me a lifetime, and I wish to hear no more."

"Destiny,"

"No!"

With a gentle moan, his mouth shut over mine, and I allowed him to close, our bodies straining to get closer. While I contented myself with being this near to him and knowing that he enjoyed being this close to me, Belial's hands gently slid into my hair, stroking and twirling it around his fingers. When we separated, he leaned his head against mine and wrapped me tighter around him while we both struggled to breathe.

"Sweetheart, please listen to me." He said in a low voice.

"I'm going to,"
"I can't stand to be by myself,"
"Belaial, you are my soul mate; I will never again let you be alone." I assured him, leaning him against me and softly petting his lovely blond hair.
"That sounds good, but bad things always happen to the people who love me. What would your parents think if a cad like me slept with their gorgeous daughter?" Belial whispered to himself.
When my parents were brought up, I started crying, and Belial's eyes got bigger when he realized I was about to cry, too.
"Oh my goodness, what did I say?" He groaned.
"My mum would have been happy that I found my soul mate because she and my dad were soul mates and they were really happy together," the twelve-year-old said of her parents before they passed away. I started to cry quietly,

unable to think about my parents since the grief I was still experiencing over their deaths made me feel so awful.

"I was unaware of that." We entered my room after he put his arms around me.

The fact that he knew where my room was startled me a little, but I didn't mind; instead, I just nuzzled into his body as he laid me down on the bed. He started to move away, assuming I wouldn't want him to sit next to me, but I sat down next to him and gripped his hand.

I felt so special as Belial's arms were wrapped around me, and we lay on the bed, just staring into each other's brown eyes and his crystal blue ones. I leaned in closer and gently pressed my lips to Belial's mouth, feeling his response till our kiss was so tender that it might have won an Oscar for any movie star! He pulled back and gave me another glance.

"Destiny, I owe you an explanation. You have a right to know why I am so cautious and afraid to love or be loved. He muttered.

"How"?

"I want to tell you about my memories."

"All right," I nodded; this would be something I had never done before, so it was rather thrilling!

Belial reached out to touch my left cheek with his hand, and I touched his right cheek in exchange, completing our physical connection. Belial then reached out to contact me with his mind. I questioned why Belial was acting this way because it was so gloomy and rather frightening in his head.

Belial offered me telepathy, making the darkness surrounding me seem to vibrate, and said, "This all happened such a long time ago, and if you want me to stop, just tell me, and I will."

I used my mind to stroke open a memory that seemed to be asking to be opened. Belial, as a tiny boy, was sitting on a worn-out carpet, playing with a small toy. He had big blue eyes and was blonde. He had been such a beautiful youngster; his mother, a young woman with brown hair who was perhaps thirty years old, was standing by the hearth and continued to stare at him lovingly. Abruptly, the door sprang open, revealing a blond man with terrified eyes.

"Anise, they've located us and are on their way!" He sobbed.

The woman quickly went to pick up Belial from the floor and then a small brunette who was sleeping on a bed.

She handed him Eden and said, "Take Eden and hide in the closet, Belial. Don't come out until papa or I tell you too."

His father ignored his pleas, "But, papa, I want to help, let me help," as he and his sister—I assume she was his sister—were hustled into the broom closet before everything went dark once more.

The following morning, I discovered them with their hearts pierced and burned, and I was powerless to save them. I believed Eden and I would be safe when we went to stay with my mother's old aunt, but I was mistaken. Belial said in my head once more as a second recollection gradually emerged.

"My boy, one day your arrogance will get you staked," said Beverly Di Aberlie. An elderly woman, who appeared to be a few years younger than the Belial I was currently with, said to one of the irresponsible vampires, "Remember that reckless humans get hurt, but a reckless vampire will be killed if his behaviour gets above him."

"Aunt Cara, stop sticking your nose where it doesn't belong. You worry about nothing. I can handle myself."

Belial informed her before leaving the house.

A young brunette remarked softly as she left the house, "Belial, she loves us and you really should respect her; she is our guardian."

"Eden, I'm going to have to settle for bothering her until I can leave this house and get married because no matter what I do, that woman will detest me." Belial yelled, causing tears to well up in the girl's light brown eyes.

I could feel his emotions, and Belial instantly regretted using such a harsh tone as he pulled the girl into his arms for an embrace. Then, there was a crash from within the home, and both of the siblings instantly looked up.

"Kids, come on over here." Despite the elderly woman's apparent agony, they turned and went back inside the house.

It's similar to when you watch a scary movie; occasionally, you yell at the TV screen, "Don't go in there, the bad guy is waiting." This was definitely one of those times when I wanted to yell at Belial and his sister to get out of the room. After falling from the stake to the ground, Belial's aunt was pushed aside by a guy wearing a black cloak. Belial pushed Eden out of the way. When the black spike brushed Eden's chest, cutting a six-inch gash in the flesh, Belial fell back and let out a yell of pain. The stake seemed to flash in the light. I witnessed Belial's transformation into a predator as he leaped to his feet and slammed the man in the cloak into the wall. He then grabbed the stake and drove it into both his abdomen and the wall behind him. He carried Eden into the woods outside the home while she was still breathing and weeping, only to have her pass away in his arms a short while later. After burying his sister, Belial returned to the cabin to burn it down and ruin the entire evening while sobbing. After the second recollection finished, I found myself attempting to wipe tears from my eyes.

Section 3: JANACLESE

I ran my fingertips over the line of silky nylon bikinis that were dangling from the metal hook. My friends and I were searching the mall for new swimwear because there were two more weeks until Miracle's pool party. Kehl-li had urged that we dress to impress and look like Sports Illustrated supermodels for the party. Didn't make sense to me because the guest list had been approved in advance by our parents. Everybody attending was either from church or school. Nobody is fresh or captivating.

My cell phone rang just as I reached for a two-piece aqua bikini.

Will you be able to obtain that?

I turned to face Cyndray and picked up a purple one-piece, pressing it up against my body. "Why? Is this one calling for Janaclese?

She arched an eyebrow. "I was referring to your cell,"

"Oh." I took my phone out of my shoulder bag and reached in. "Hey?"

"Do you drive?" Mom enquired.

I took a deep breath. "No, mother. I'm still out shopping.

"I didn't think a single purchase would take the entire day. You told me you were with someone, but who?

"Cyndray, Miracle, and Kehl-li." Why did she always make me go through this bothersome process as if she didn't already know?

I could see that Cyndray was enjoying our chat by the lighthearted expression in her eyes. However, I didn't think it was funny that my mother was asking how I was doing, especially since

Cyndray had called me "Your Righteousness."

"Hi Mrs. M!" Cyndray took the bathing suit from me and attempted to shout into the phone. "You have to see your daughter taking a hot bath."

After hitting the mute button, I pushed Cyndray out of my way. Mom was not amused by her jokes. She would call off our celebration and instead teach us the value of modesty. "Will you please stop playing around?"

Cyndray laughed. "Your mother forbids you from leaving the house in that tiny bikini."

"Is Cyndray shouting in the background?" Across the phone, Mom sounded earnest. "What's on trend?"

I turned off the mute and held the phone up to my ear, scowling at Cyndray. Nothing at all Other than the summer heat that's making my hair poufy;

nothing is hot. Did you need me to come home and conduct an errand?

"No, but after you drop your friends off, I need you to come straight home."

I rolled my eyes. You don't have to inquire as to why. Indeed. Alright.

"And let me know when you're headed over." One another of Mom's peculiar rules for parenting.

I said, "Yeah. Okay," and then clicked away.

I attempted to take the bikini off of Cyndray. "I was merely observing it." In addition, my mother is unaware of what is behind my clothing.

"Mrs. Mitchell? She's always one step ahead of everyone, huh? If she was wearing espionage gear under that bathing suit, it wouldn't surprise me. She made contact with the cloth and tags while feigning to look for a concealed camera. Perhaps that explains why she called as soon as you removed this miserable item from the rack.

Kehl-li wrinkled her nose at Cyndray's purple one-piece after only a glance. It appears that you were unable to locate anything valuable either. We ought to check out a designer store.

Not everyone is as wealthy as you are. Purchasing swimwear is a luxury with my summer salary. Cyndray extended the bathing suit I had chosen. This belongs to Janaclese. Do you enjoy it?

Kehl-li tossed her long, straight, dark hair, not wanting to touch the clothes, as if she was afraid she could pick up an unclean look. She cast a menacing glance at me. "Do you want to impress your boyfriend by buying that?"

I felt a tingling sensation go down my cheeks, thinking of Hassan in spite of myself. I gave a headshake. "You are aware that I am single."

Kehl-li creased her face tightly. "So what's the purpose?"

"Why are boys at the centre of everything you think about?" Cyndray regarded Kehl-li with icy eyes. "You don't even have a boyfriend yourself, despite how much you think you know."

There was no way that the two could share the same air without fighting. Miracle waved her fingers rapidly around the tail of her cotton shirt as her eyes flicked back and forth between Cyndray and Kehl-li. The muscles in my stomach twitched, too. Neither my friends nor my parents could tolerate arguing.

"I can get a guy before you do, Betcha!" Kehl-li put Cyndray to the test.

Miracle took the rumpled shirttail out of her grip. "You would not win. She has already started dating the most attractive student.

"You're in a relationship?" Kehl-li gave Cyndray a squint.

"I am not Trevor's boyfriend." Cyndray stood quite still, staring down at the tiled floor.

"You're not in a relationship with the hottest boy at school?" Kehl-li has glittering eyes. "So he's available for grabs?"

Cyndray's calm exterior didn't fool me. A spark with her may start an explosion. I moved gently between Cyndray and Kehl-li. Trevor is not for sale. You speak of him as though he were a piece of meat.

Cyndray evaded me in an attempt to confront Kehl-li. "You can have Trevor if you believe you can get him."

"Is that a challenge?" Kehl-li combed a lock of straight black hair off her face, which was naturally tanned.

What is the Korean phrase for "no"? Cyndray's nose widened. Since you don't appear to comprehend English

"Aniyo," declared Miracle. "In Korean, aniyo means no."

Cyndray gave Miracle a frustrated glance before hurling himself at Kehl-li. "I'm not challenging you, Aniyo. Trevor isn't my boyfriend, Aniyo. I can't afford boutique prices, Aniyo.

Kehl-li gave a sneer. "Temper, indeed?"

"Aniyo-contrary!" My swimsuit was thrown across the rack by Cyndray. "Leave now."

"Cyndray, hold on!" I watched my friend rush off with the one-piece in her hand, grabbing the bikini before it struck the floor. Kehl-li appeared to take pleasure in infuriating Cyndray. Was that required? You are aware of her nature.

Kehl-li stared beyond me and pointed at Miracle, her sly lips spreading into a broad smile. Is that not Hassan, MiCha?

Hassan? At the sound of the name, my stomach lurched. Is that possible?

As I turned to face Kehl-li's index finger, my heart began to race. The beating seemed like it might blow up my chest. It was him, the VBS guy. Please keep him from seeing me.

"MiCha, hurry up and let's go speak with him." Kehl-li reached for Miracle's hand and gestured while yelling his name.

Looking over, Hassan squinted and smiled toothily, giving me the impression that I had never seen him before. While working on the swimsuit, I managed to get a few glimpses of him conversing with Miracle and Kehl-li. A part of me hoped I possessed Kehl-li's bravery, and another part of me wanted to hide between the clothing rack. However, given the way I landed on top of him, he most likely felt I was strange. It hadn't helped either that Mrs. Dunning had swept me out of the room. A disturbing notion raced across my mind, and I gripped the rack with both hands. What if I was forgotten by him? That would be considerably more detrimental.

I glanced over the rack and met Hassan's gaze; he turned to face me. Hangers clattered on the floor as my slick hands tilted the bar forward.

Stretching out, Hassan balanced the rack. "You mean Janaclese?"

Our focus was taken away by the alarm going off in the store.

"Avoid touching me!" Cyndray's arms were flailing away from a security guard as her eyes sprung open like two round bagels coming out of a hot toaster near the store's exit. "I didn't steal anything! Take your hands off me!

My legs froze while my heart pounded into overdrive. How were we going to tell my mother this?